BENEATH THE STONE

BENEATH THE STONE
◼ A MEXICAN ZAPOTEC TALE ◼

WRITTEN AND PHOTOGRAPHED BY BERNARD WOLF

ORCHARD BOOKS
New York

ACKNOWLEDGMENTS

My deepest gratitude goes to Leo, his brothers, Ruben and Abrán, his sister, Susana,
and his parents, Lucio and Antonieta, for their unfailing trust, hospitality, and cooperation;
to Lorenzo Gutierrez Lopez of Teotitlán del Valle, who taught me so much about the history of his village;
to Marcela Taboada, photographer, and Héctor Jara, her artist husband, of Oaxaca City,
who gave me encouragement, friendship, and assistance when I most needed it;
finally, to Neal Porter and Maggie Herold, my editors, and to Sallie Baldwin, my designer.

ORCHARD BOOKS
95 MADISON AVENUE, NEW YORK, NY 10016

Manufactured in Singapore   Printed and bound by Toppan Printing Company, Inc.

BOOK DESIGN BY ANTLER & BALDWIN DESIGN GROUP

10 9 8 7 6 5 4 3 2 1

The text of this book is set in 16 point Zapf International Light. All of the pictures in this book were made with Nikon equipment.
I used F4 and 8008 S bodies. My lenses were a 24mm AF F2.8, a 28mm F2, a 35mm AF F2, an 85 mm AF F1.8, and an 80 to 200mm AF/ED F2.8 zoom.
My film was professional Fujichrome 100. The four-color separations were reproduced from the original full-color transparencies.

Library of Congress Cataloging-in-Publication Data

Wolf, Bernard, date.
    Beneath the stone : a Mexican Zapotec tale / written and photographed by Bernard Wolf.
        p. cm.
    Summary: The customs and daily life of a small village in Oaxaca, Mexico, are shown
through the eyes of a six-year-old Zapotec Indian boy.
    ISBN 0-531-06835-8. — ISBN 0-531-08685-2 (lib. bdg.)
    1. Zapotec Indians—Juvenile literature. 2. Teotitlán del Valle (Mexico)—Social life and
customs—Juvenile literature. 3. Mexico—Juvenile literature. [1. Zapotec Indians. 2. Indians
of Mexico. 3. Mexico—Social life and customs.] I. Title.
F1221.Z3W65 1994
972'.74—dc20   92-27103

Shamefully, I cannot recall or find her name now,
but there have been countless times when
I have blessed her memory, her spirit, and her gift.
She was my high school Spanish teacher.

About 3,500 years ago a band of wanderers walked from the north of what is now Mexico until they came to a beautiful mountain valley. The weary travelers liked this place so much that they decided to stay. They called themselves Zapotec. With them they carried the image of their most important god, Teos. If they felt tired, they reasoned, their god must also be tired. So they placed the image beneath a stone to rest.

Today their ancient settlement is called Teotitlán del Valle. This means "Beneath the Stone in the Valley."

The village lies in the Oaxaca Valley, 350 miles south of Mexico City. This is where a young Zapotec Indian boy lives. His name is Leodegario Vicente Golan Ruiz, but everyone calls him Leo. Leo is six years old. He and his people are weavers of tapetes, which are used as rugs or wall hangings. Their work is famous throughout Mexico.

Leo's eleven-year-old sister, Susana

His father, Lucio

Eulalia, his ninety-nine-year-old great-grandmother, and Abrán, his fourteen-year-old brother

Leo also has a seventeen-year-old brother, Joaquín, who lives and works in California. He is going to have an eye operation. Tomorrow morning everyone will go to the village church to pray for

His mother, Antonieta

Ruben, his eighteen-year-old brother

him. Ruben lived in California for one year, but he has a novia, a sweetheart, here. She is sixteen years old. They plan to marry in two years. Eulalia lives in her own house nearby. ◨

Leo's breakfast is a bowl of atole, a vegetable soup with green corn, sugar, salt, and chili sauce. His brother Abrán and sister Susana go to school from 8:00 A.M. to 1:30 P.M. His parents and Ruben have been working since sunrise. While there isn't much money to buy him toys, Leo is a happy boy. He has the love and warmth of his family and he is never bored. Everyone works, even Leo. Every morning his mother helps him practice his weaving. Leo told his parents that he wanted to weave when he was five years old. Because of his youth they were surprised, but pleased. Now he weaves small tapetes in simple patterns.

Weaving a tapete is complicated. It takes almost a week just to prepare the wool. This work is done in the large earthen courtyard of the house.

First the yarn is washed to remove dirt and oil. Next the wool is cooked in a big pot of boiling water and dye. Each color requires a different pot of dye. The dyed yarn is then hung in the sun to dry. Later each color must be untangled and wound onto spools ready for weaving.

Finally Leo's father attaches vertical strands of washed white wool to the looms. The colored yarns will be woven across them.

Lucio is worried. Business has been poor. The family's supply of costly wool and dyes is running low, as is their money. Still, he must buy new materials. The Christmas season is approaching. Then he expects more and bigger sales and he wants to be prepared for them. But first he must earn some money. Tonight he will search again in Oaxaca City for customers. ◼

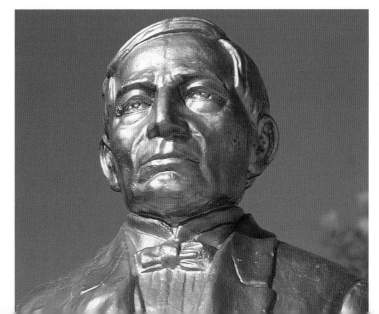

Leo goes to school in the afternoons from one-thirty until six. His school is named after Benito Juárez. In the courtyard stands a golden statue of this beloved man. Juárez was a humble Zapotec Indian who became Mexico's greatest president.

Leo's first grade teacher is Mrs. Matías. She teaches her class to read, write, and speak Spanish. This is not easy for Leo and his classmates, because all the villagers speak ancient Zapotec. But Zapotec is not a written language. For Leo learning to read is an adventure. He wants to discover what the black marks in books mean. He wants to be a weaver

like his father, but he also wants to study. Before dismissing her class, Mrs. Matías announces that they must all prepare for an important fiesta, festival, in three weeks.

Leo discusses this with his best compadre, pal, Luis. Luis lives in the house next to Leo's. In their free time the boys invent games to play with pebbles, sticks, and an old soccer ball.

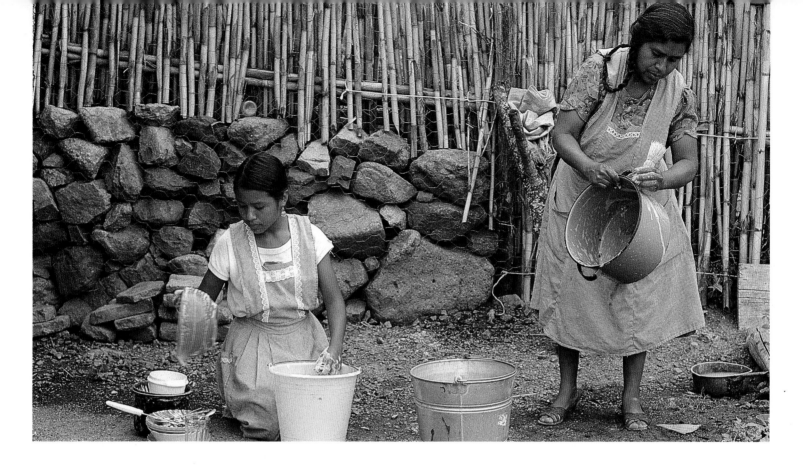

 Fiestas and religion play major roles in Mexican Indian life. Leo and his family are devout Catholics, but before the Spaniards came in 1519, the Zapotecs prayed to many gods. Some ancient beliefs persist.

November 1 begins Los Dias de los Muertos, The Days of the Dead. The Zapotecs believe that, for two days each year, the spirits of the dead return to visit their loved ones. With help from Susana, Antonieta makes tamales for the many guests who will share her family's nightlong vigil. When she and Susana have finished, they wash the pots in the courtyard.

Leo's father strings up colorful lights above the family's altar. Electricity is expensive, but this is a special occasion. Antonieta arranges flowers, water, and loaves of bread before the altar's santos, saints. When the spirits arrive, they will be hungry and thirsty. Then she burns copal, the ancient incense of the Mexican Indians, and prays silently. She and her husband have seen strange things during these days. Once Lucio saw the shadow of a man walk through a wall of his house and vanish!

After dark Leo's aunt Guadalupe and her husband arrive, bringing bread for the altar. Everyone is cheerful. Later the family goes to call on other relatives. These visits continue all night, and Leo can stay up as long as he likes!

The next afternoon the villagers place flowers and fruit on the graves of their dead. The spirits will depart when night falls. ◫

November 20 is an exciting day for Leo and his classmates, and for Mexico. It is the anniversary of the Mexican Revolution, a day when, in 1910, the Indians and peasants of Mexico took up arms against a corrupt government and the ruthless landowners who had kept them in poverty for centuries. Their desperate struggle ended in victory. In 1920 Mexico became a democratic republic.

Leo and his classmates wear period costumes. They will march in the big parade through the village this morning. Leo pretends he is Emiliano Zapata, one of the heroes of the Revolution. Mrs. Matías paints and glues mustaches on the faces of her boys, then rushes to form up her class.

Proud mothers line the dusty streets of Teotitlán. The band strikes up a lively tune, and the parade begins!

♫ The week before Christmas is a very busy time for Leo and his family. The only money they earn is from selling their tapetes. Lucio's best sales are made in July, August, and especially December, when visitors from all around Mexico and the world come to see Oaxaca's colorful fiestas.

For two weeks Ruben has been weaving an extra-large tapete. But today is Friday, and Lucio wants it finished for tomorrow's market in the city. On Sunday he plans to go to another market as well, so father and son work at the same loom.

By late afternoon the tapete is completed. Antonieta has just finished three new tapetes, each one a different design, and Leo adds another small tapete to these. Everyone wishes for good luck this weekend. Leo is excited about going to the city! ▟

The 7:00 A.M. bus carries Leo and his parents through mountains to the city, twenty-five miles away. It is a forty-five-minute trip. Oaxaca City is the capital of the state of Oaxaca. Each Saturday morning thousands of Zapotec Indians from mountain villages flock here to the Mercado de Abastos, the biggest market in Mexico. This is where Leo and his parents come each week to display and sell their woven goods. After arranging

his stall, Lucio shows Leo how he'll make a shoulder bag from Leo's small tapete. He knots the hanging strands to seal the sides. Later he'll sew on a long strap.

The market is a good meeting place for friends. A neighbor stops by to visit.

Across the alley in a basket weaver's stall, a young girl pouts as her mother braids her hair.

Antonieta will do her big weekly shopping this morning. She takes Leo with her to help carry her purchases.

Leo loves the colors, sounds, and smells of the market. Everywhere cries of "Compra! Es barato!"—"Buy! Its cheap!"—ring through the air. All kinds of food is sold here, including fried grasshoppers! Women sit among huge mounds of fruit and vegetables.

A young girl heaps grilled meat onto tortillas for hungry customers. Antonieta buys two of these, which she and Leo munch as they shop.

No Mexican would cook without chili peppers. Antonieta buys a variety of these, from mild to fiery hot.

Back at the stall, tourists come to inspect the tapetes. One of them buys Leo's shoulder bag! But by the end of the day Lucio has sold only two of his wife's tapetes for 120,000 pesos each. In American money this is a total of eighty dollars. He doesn't feel that's much money for all the work that went into them.

On Sunday Lucio's luck is better. At the second largest market town, Tlacolula, where he has another selling space, a Canadian and his wife are attracted to Ruben's large tapete. After much bargaining Lucio sells it for 800,000 pesos—$266.00! Antonieta buys three chickens for a Christmas Day feast. Then she and Leo rush home before dark.

For the people of Teotitlán, Christmas is a solemn time. Every night, from December 15 until Christmas Eve, there is a candelit procession through the dark streets of the village. Tonight, for the first time, Leo joins a Posada de los Peregrinos, Procession of the Pilgrims, with his mother.

Four maidens carry the images of Mary and Joseph, who seek shelter for the birth of the infant Jesus. This is what happened on a cold night in Bethlehem long ago.

The procession stops at house after house. Each time the pilgrims beg for shelter, but the door remains locked to them. Finally, one door opens.

Leo watches in awe as the images are carried in and placed on the altar.

The air is filled with copal incense. There is deep longing for the birth of the Christ child.

Business has improved for Lucio. With the holidays behind him, he keeps a promise he made to Leo.

High on a mountain near Oaxaca City lies the ancient capital of the Zapotecs, Monte Albán. Built around 500 B.C., it was one of the first cities in the Americas.

His father has told Leo that the Zapotecs leveled the entire top of this mountain to build this city. How did they do that? he wonders. No one knows.

Holding his father's hand, Leo, his brother Abrán, and his mother climb the steep steps to the top of a temple. While Leo looks around in wonder, Lucio tells him that from this city their ancestors ruled a rich and powerful kingdom. From this mountaintop one can see the tallest mountain above Teotitlán. It is believed that, either by signal fire or reflected light, the ancestors "spoke" to the Place Beneath the Stone. Once 25,000 people lived here. Now there is only silence and these remarkable stone buildings from the past.

Antonieta unpacks the breakfast she has brought. The food they eat this morning is not different from the food eaten here so long ago—corn tortillas, beans, eggs, green squash, and chili peppers.

Leo has been given much to think about, but he will not forget the old stories of his people. Perhaps one day he will bring his own son to this place of mystery and memories. ◪

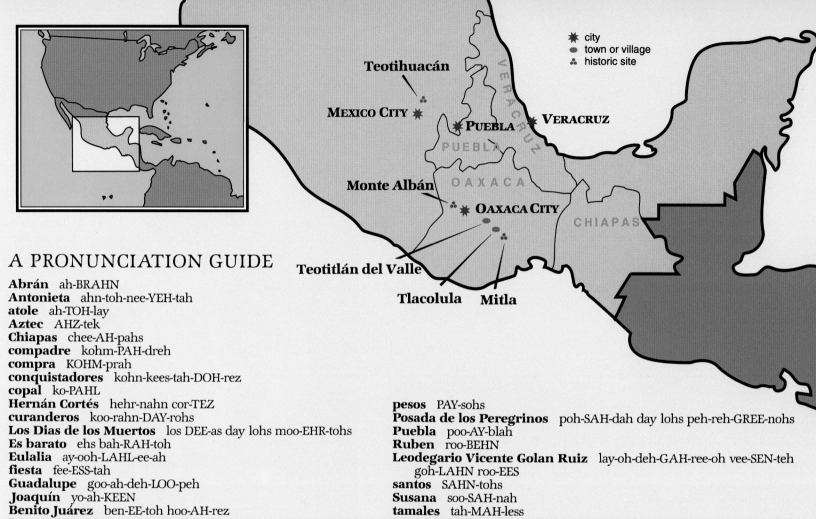

Teotihuacán

MEXICO CITY

PUEBLA VERACRUZ

★ city
● town or village
♣ historic site

Monte Albán

OAXACA CITY

Teotitlán del Valle

Tlacolula Mitla

A PRONUNCIATION GUIDE

Abrán ah-BRAHN
Antonieta ahn-toh-nee-YEH-tah
atole ah-TOH-lay
Aztec AHZ-tek
Chiapas chee-AH-pahs
compadre kohm-PAH-dreh
compra KOHM-prah
conquistadores kohn-kees-tah-DOH-rez
copal ko-PAHL
Hernán Cortés hehr-nahn cor-TEZ
curanderos koo-rahn-DAY-rohs
Los Dias de los Muertos los DEE-as day lohs moo-EHR-tohs
Es barato ehs bah-RAH-toh
Eulalia ay-ooh-LAHL-ee-ah
fiesta fee-ESS-tah
Guadalupe goo-ah-deh-LOO-peh
Joaquín yo-ah-KEEN
Benito Juárez ben-EE-toh hoo-AH-rez
Leo LAY-o
Lucio loo-SEE-oh
Luis loo-EES
Mrs. Matías mah-TEE-ahs
Maya MAH-yah
Mercado de Abastos mer-KAH-doh day ah-BAH-stohs
Mitla MEET-lah
Moctezuma mok-teh-ZOO-mah
Monte Albán mohn-tay ahl-BAHN
novia NOH-vee-ah
Oaxaca wha-HAH-kah
Olmec OHL-mek

pesos PAY-sohs
Posada de los Peregrinos poh-SAH-dah day lohs peh-reh-GREE-nohs
Puebla poo-AY-blah
Ruben roo-BEHN
Leodegario Vicente Golan Ruiz lay-oh-deh-GAH-ree-oh vee-SEN-teh goh-LAHN roo-EES
santos SAHN-tohs
Susana soo-SAH-nah
tamales tah-MAH-less
tapetes tah-PAY-tays
Tenochtitlán tek-nok-teet-LAHN
Teos TAY-ohs
Teotihuacán tay-oh-tee-hwah-KAHN
Teotitlán del Valle teh-o-teet-LAHN del VAHL-yeh
Tlacolula tlah-koh-LOO-lah
Toltec TOHL-tek
tortillas tor-TEE-ahs
Totonac toh-TOH-nak
Veracruz vehr-ah-CROOZ
Emiliano Zapata em-eel-YAH-noh zah-PAH-tah
Zapotec ZAH-poh-tek

Mexican history stretches back more than 12,000 years. Between 1200 B.C. and A.D. 900, while much of Europe lived in a primitive state, great civilizations developed and flourished here—Olmec, Toltec, Zapotec, Totonac, Maya, and Aztec.

The Zapotecs raised an impressive culture in the Oaxaca Valley. Their principal cities were Monte Albán and Mitla. These cities show the artistic and mathematical genius of the Zapotecs, who developed a bar-and-dot numerical system and a fifty-two-cycle yearly calendar. Their political and economic power reached as far as Chiapas, Veracruz, Puebla, and Teotihuacán, and their military prowess withstood even the onslaught of the mighty Aztec war machine.

In 1519 the first Spaniards arrived, a band of four hundred adventurers led by Hernán Cortés. Using superstition, treachery, and shrewd strategy, Cortés overthrew the superior forces of the Aztec emperor Moctezuma at Tenochtitlán (Mexico City). His appetite whetted by Aztec gold, Cortés, with reinforcements from Spain, marched south in search of further treasure. Despite fierce resistance, Cortés, with his superior weapons and tactics, overcame all native opposition to become the conqueror of New Spain.

In the wake of the conquistadores came Spanish priests and missionaries bringing Catholicism. The great ancient cities and temples were destroyed. In their place the Spaniards constructed churches, cathedrals, and towns, using the slave labor of the Indians. The Spaniards also brought smallpox, typhus, and cholera, which killed 50 to 90 percent of the native inhabitants. They then divided among themselves all of the richest lands, leaving the surviving Indians to live in appalling poverty for the next four hundred years.

It was not until the Revolution of 1910–1920 that Mexico finally shook off its legacy of foreign and Spanish oppression. A major land reform was enforced, returning to the peasants and Indians land stolen from them by the church and corrupt landowners.

Today Mexico has emerged from a "developing nation" status to become Latin America's most dynamic democratic republic. The lot of its diverse Indian cultures has vastly improved. In spite of lingering racial prejudice, these people are treated with some respect now. Most importantly, they are left to pursue their own life-styles and traditions.

The Zapotecs live in hundreds of villages throughout the Oaxaca Valley. By valley standards, Leo's village is considered prosperous. Unlike many of its neighbors, whose economy depends on farming, Teotitlán's economy rests upon the skill of its weavers. Other villages are famous for their pottery, woodcarvings, silver jewelry, et cetera.

While the federal government of Mexico provides and runs free schools in the villages, it has no political authority within them. Each village functions as an autonomous unit. In Teotitlán all important communal decisions are made by its municipal committee led by a headman, according to ancient custom.

There are five doctors and a medical clinic in the village, but many villagers still prefer the services of curanderos, medicine men. It is common for people to live to the age of ninety and beyond. Clean air, healthy diet, plus the non-use of tobacco and coffee may contribute toward this.

Very few homes possess modern plumbing. The water used in Leo's house comes from a mountain spring high above the village. It flows through buried pipes to his home and is stored in a big metal tank in the courtyard. There is no bathroom in Leo's house. He bathes by pouring pans of cold water over his soapy body. The family's toilet is a hole in the ground behind the house.

Teotitlán's rough stone and earth streets remain unpaved, as they always have been. With its population of 10,000, there is only one public telephone in the village. Yet most families, including Leo's, own refrigerators, butane gas stoves, color TVs, and VCRs. Not many people own automobiles, but these too are on the increase. In spite of all this, the Zapotecs remain strongly bonded to their cultural heritage and traditions. They are not disinterested in the outside world, but their loyalties remain deeply rooted in their families and their community.